This edition first published in 2001 by Macmillan Children's Books
Originally published in 1997 as
The Silent Beetle Eats the Seeds, Proverbs from Far and Wide
by Macmillan Children's Books
A division of Macmillan Publishers Limited
20 New Wharf Road, London, N1 9RR
Basingstoke and Oxford
Associated companies throughout the world
www.macmillan.com

ISBN 0 333 96128 5

Text copyright © 2001 Macmillan Children's Books
Illustrations copyright © 1997 Axel Scheffler
Moral rights asserted

1 3 5 7 9 8 6 4 2

A CIP catalogue record for this book is available from the British Library.

Printed in Belgium by Proost.

Axel Scheffler

Proverbs from Far and Wide

MACMILLAN CHILDREN'S BOOKS

FRIEND OR FOE?
Proverbs about Friendship

Birds in their
little nests
agree.

England

Monkeys pick fruit together.

Liberia

A hedge between keeps
friendships green.

France

The cat and dog may kiss,
but are they friends?

If you step on one ant,
the others come
to bite you too.

West Africa

Two sparrows on one ear of corn
make an ill agreement.

If two men quarrel, even
their dogs have a difference.

Japan

MIRROR, MIRROR ON THE WALL

Proverbs about How You Look

If the baboon could see his own behind,
he would laugh too.

Kenya

The monkey has a big mouth because, he says, otherwise he would be too pretty.

Ewe

The polecat does not know it stinks.

Zulu

He that has a big nose thinks everyone speaks of it.

Scotland

A chicken with beautiful plumage does not sit in a corner.

West Africa

It is only when the cold season comes that we know the pine and cypress to be evergreens.

China

BE PREPARED!

*Proverbs about Being in the Right Place
at the Right Time*

Where you hear there are plenty of cherries,
always carry a small basket.

Greece

The silent beetle
eats the seeds.

Tanzania

The frog saw the horse being shod
and presented his feet also.

Turkey

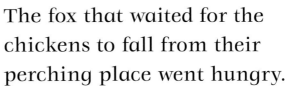

The fox that waited for the
chickens to fall from their
perching place went hungry.

Greece

The early bird
catches the worm.

WHAT HAPPENS NEXT?

Proverbs about Consequences

Those who have one foot in the canoe
and one foot in the boat are going to
fall in the river.

Tuscarora

If you have a monkey under
your blanket, it will move
and make a bulge.

South Africa

He that steals honey should
watch out for the sting.

China

If the camel gets his nose in the
tent, his body will soon follow.

Arabia

An arrow shot upright falls
on the shooter's head.

IN A MINUTE!

Proverbs about Being Patient

The monkey learns to jump
by trying again and again.

West Africa

He that would have eggs must endure the cackling of hens.

Greece

A watched pot never boils.

Hair by hair, you may pluck out the whole beard.

Russia

A hasty man drinks tea with his fork.

India

THAT'S THE WAY THE COOKIE CRUMBLES

Proverbs about Luck

The heaviest
rains fall on
the leakiest
house.

Japan

If I peddle salt, it rains;
if I peddle flour,
the wind blows.

Japan

If you throw a handful of stones,
at least one will hit.

India

Throw him in the river and
he will rise with a fish
in his mouth.

Arabia

The tortoise's food is eaten
by others. Without quick
legs, what can he do?

Zambia

While a man is driving a tiger
away from his front door,
a wolf is entering the back.

China

THAT'S NOT FAIR!

Proverbs about Injustice

The smallest boy always
carries the biggest fiddle.

England

A fox should not be on
the jury at a goose's trial.

England

The cat steals the rice and
the dog comes and eats it.

China

The worst hog often gets
the best pear.

Italy

An ox with long horns,
even if he does not butt,
will be accused of butting.

Malay

LOOK OUT!

Proverbs about Being Careful

When the fox preaches, keep an eye on your geese.

Germany

If you take the wrong hat from the meeting, make sure it doesn't belong to a big man.

Ireland

When two hippopotamuses quarrel, don't put your oar in.

Buganda

Do not speak of secrets in a field that is full of little hills.

Hebrew

Look before you leap.

England

Let sleeping dogs lie.

England

rust in God, but tie your camel.

Persia

I WANT WHAT YOU'VE GOT!

 *Proverbs about Envy*

When everyone praised the peacock for his beautiful tail,
the birds cried out together, "But look at his legs
and what a voice!"

Japan

The cow from afar gives plenty of milk.

France

Our neighbour's crop seems better than our own.

Latin

The grass is always greener on the other side of the fence.

He who gives to others' dogs is barked at by his own.

Italy

Your neighbour's apples are the sweetest.

Yiddish

WHO KNOWS BEST?

Proverbs about Wisdom

The giraffe is wise:
he never makes a
noise and he can
see far away.

Tanzania

The tortoise is the wisest.
He carries his own home.

Bambara

If there were wisdom in beards,
all goats would be prophets.

Armenia

A foolish man waters an elephant
with a spoon.

Persia

The hen with
a worm in its bill
will not cackle.

Wise is the man who
has two loaves, and
sells one to buy a lily.

China

The old elephant knows
where to find water.

South Africa

LEARN FROM YOUR MISTAKES

Proverbs about Experience

Only when you have crossed the river
can you say the crocodile has a lump
on his snout.

Ashanti

Only the wearer knows
where the shoe pinches.

England

Don't sit on the horse's nose
no matter how much you know
about horses.

Bambara

He who has been
bitten by a snake
fears a piece
of string.

Persia

To know the road ahead,
ask those coming back.

China

THAT'S JUST SILLY!

Proverbs about Impossible Things

You cannot find a striped squirrel
in every hollow fence pole.

North America

You cannot make a
crab walk straight.

Greek

Two watermelons cannot
be held in one hand.

Persia

The cow cannot
jump about
the tree like
a squirrel.

Germany

You cannot catch lions
with cobwebs.

North America

Frowning frogs cannot stop the
cow drinking from the pool.

Kikuyu

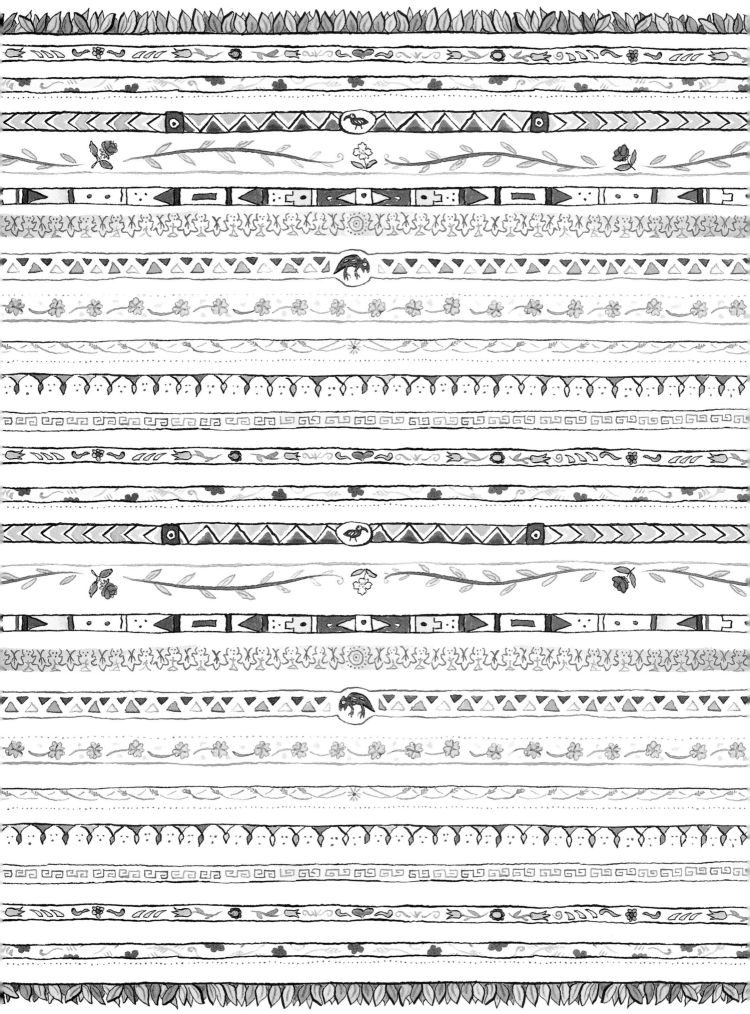